FOND DU LAC PUBLIC LIBRARY

WITHDRAWN

D1514749

Sea Turtles

By Valerie J. Weber

Reading Consultant: Susan Nations, M.Ed.,
author/literacy coach/consultant in literacy development

WEEKLY READER®
PUBLISHING

Please visit our web site at www.garethstevens.com.
For a free catalog describing our list of high-quality books,
call 1-800-542-2595 (USA) or 1-800-387-3178 (Canada).
Our fax: 1-877-542-2596

Library of Congress Cataloging-in-Publication Data

Weber, Valerie.
     Sea turtles / by Valerie J. Weber.
        p. cm. — (Animals that live in the ocean)
     Includes bibliographical references and index.
     ISBN-10: 0-8368-9244-5   ISBN-13: 978-0-8368-9244-4 (lib. bdg.)
     ISBN-10: 0-8368-9343-3   ISBN-13: 978-0-8368-9343-4 (softcover)
     1. Sea turtles—Juvenile literature. I. Title.
  QL666.C536W43   2009
  597.92'8—dc22   2008013546

This edition first published in 2009 by
Weekly Reader® Books
An Imprint of Gareth Stevens Publishing
1 Reader's Digest Road
Pleasantville, NY 10570-7000 USA

Copyright © 2009 by Gareth Stevens, Inc.

Senior Managing Editor: Lisa M. Herrington
Senior Editor: Barbara Bakowski
Creative Director: Lisa Donovan
Designer: Alexandria Davis
Cover Designer: Amelia Favazza, *Studio Montage*
Photo Researcher: Diane Laska-Swanke

Photo Credits: Cover © Georgette Douwma/Getty Images;
pp. 1, 5, 7, 9, 11, 13, 15, 17, 19, 21 © SeaPics.com

Printed in the United States of America

1 2 3 4 5 6 7 8 9 10 09 08

Table of Contents

Boldface words appear in the glossary.

A Long Journey

A female sea turtle swims
through the sea. She flaps
her front flippers like wings.
Her back flippers help
her steer.

front flippers

back flippers

She swims hundreds of miles to the beach where she was born. Why does she travel so far? Sea turtles return to their home beach to lay eggs.

A Hard Task

The sea turtle pulls herself out of the water. She then crawls to a dry patch of sand. Using her flippers, she digs a hole.

9

The female sea turtle lays her eggs in the hole. Then she covers the eggs with sand. She is hiding them from **predators** that want to eat the eggs.

eggs

After a few weeks, baby turtles **hatch**, or break out of the eggs. They dig their way out of the sand.

Then the baby sea turtles head for the ocean. They must move fast! Birds and crabs may try to eat them.

Bodies Built for the Sea

A baby turtle looks just like an adult turtle. A **shell** protects most of its body. **Scales** cover the shells of most sea turtles.

scales

shell

17

Nostrils, or holes for breathing, are at the top of the turtle's head. The turtle does not have to lift its whole head out of the water to breathe.

nostrils

Different kinds of sea turtles eat different kinds of food. The leatherback turtle eats soft jellyfish. The loggerhead turtle has a sharp **beak** that helps it eat crabs and lobsters.

loggerhead turtle

lobster

Glossary

beak: a hard, pointed mouth

hatch: to break out of an egg

nostrils: a pair of holes on the head through which an animal breathes

predators: animals that hunt and eat other animals

scales: thin, flat, hard plates that cover a turtle's shell

shell: a hard outer covering that protects the body of an animal

For More Information

Books

Baby Sea Turtle. Nature Babies (series).
Aubrey Lang (Fitzhenry and Whiteside, 2007)

Sea Turtles. Let's Read About Animals (series).
Kathleen Pohl (Weekly Reader Early Learning Library, 2007)

Web Sites

Sea Turtles at Enchanted Learning
www.enchantedlearning.com/subjects/turtle/
Seaturtlecoloring.shtml
Color in a diagram of a sea turtle, and learn more
about sea turtles' lives.

Shedd Aquarium: Green Sea Turtle
www.sheddaquarium.org/greenseaturtle.html
Explore the life of a green sea turtle, and find
out why it is green.

Publisher's note to educators and parents: Our editors have carefully reviewed these web sites to ensure that they are suitable for children. Many web sites change frequently, however, and we cannot guarantee that a site's future contents will continue to meet our high standards of quality and educational value. Be advised that children should be closely supervised whenever they access the Internet.

Index

About the Author

A writer and editor for 25 years, Valerie Weber especially loves working in children's publishing. The variety of topics is endless, from weird animals to making movies. It is her privilege to try to engage children in their world through books.